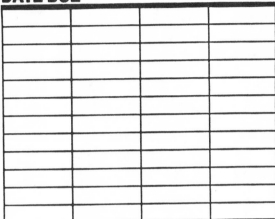

DATE DUE

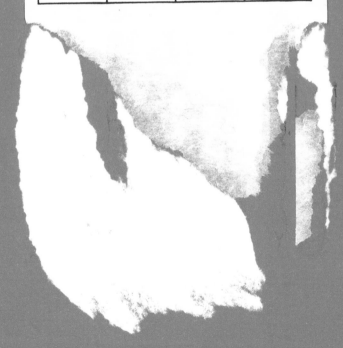

Creepy Creatures

Earthworms

Sue Barraclough

Chicago, Illinois

For information, address the publisher:
Raintree, 100 N. LaSalle, Suite 1200, Chicago, IL 60602

Printed and bound in China by South China Printing Company.
09 08 07 06 05
10 9 8 7 6 5 4 3 2 1

Library of Congress Cataloging-in-Publication Data
A copy of the cataloging-in-publication data for this title is on file with the Library of Congress.
  Earthworms/ Sue Barraclough
  ISBN 1-4109-1506-9 (HC), 1-4109-1511-5 (Pbk.)

Acknowledgments
The publisher would like to thank the following for permission to reproduce copyright material: Alamy Images pp.8-9 (Maximillian Weinzieri), 19 (Papilio); Ardea pp. 4, 16, 17 (Steve Hopkin); Corbis pp.14-15 (Robin Chittenden; Frank Lane Picture Agency), 21 (Joe McDonald), 20 (Lightscapes Photography Inc.); Ecoscene pp.6 (Wayne Lawler), 10-11 (Robert Pickett) FLPA p.12, 13 (David Hosking); Holt Studios International Ltd pp.7 top, 23; Oxford Scientific Films pp. 18 (Kathie Atkinson), 22 (David M Dennis); Science Photo Library p.7 bottom (Dr Morley Read).

Cover photograph reproduced with permission of Ardea/ Steve Hopkin.

Every effort has been made to contact copyright holders of any material reproduced in this book. Any omissions will be rectified in subsequent printings if notice is given to the publisher.

Some words are shown in bold, **like this**. You can find out what they mean by looking in the glossary on page 24.

Contents

Earthworms

Earthworms are small animals with **LONG**, soft bodies.

Types of Earthworms

Many different kinds of worms
live in **soil** and in water.

Looking for Earthworms

You might see earthworms in the **soil** in a garden.

When the soil is wet, they **wriggle** through it.

An Earthworm's Body

An earthworm's long body is divided into **segments.**

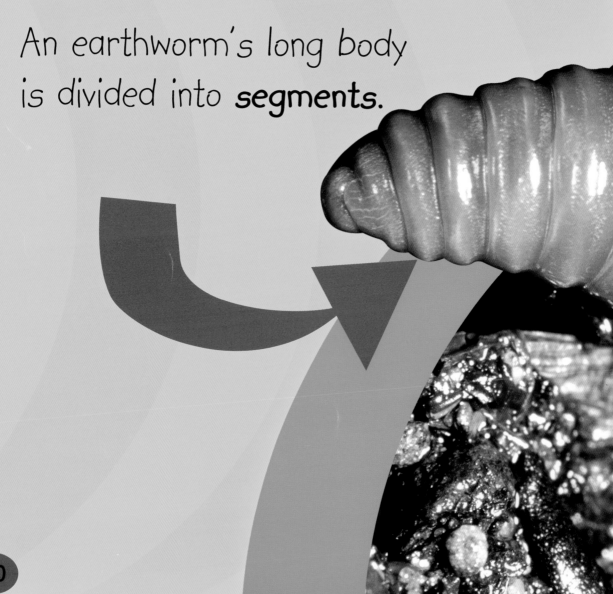

An earthworm does not have
a real head or any legs.

How Earthworms Move

To move, an earthworm **stretches** and pushes forward.

This makes its body **LONG** and thin...

... and then it pulls
its tail end forward.

Laying Eggs

It takes two earthworms to make eggs.

Earthworms' Eggs

Each egg has a hard case called a **cocoon**. The cocoon protects the egg as it grows.

When it is ready, the tiny worm
pushes its way out of the egg.

Food for Earthworms

Earthworms pull dead leaves into their **burrows** to eat.

18

worm castings

Worm **castings** are what is left of an earthworm's meal!

Earthworms in Danger

Many different kinds of animals like to eat earthworms.

Earthworms use **bristles** on their bodies to try to keep themselves from being pulled out of the **soil**.

Useful Earthworms

The holes earthworms make let air into the **soil** and let water drain out.

Worms eat many kinds of waste.

This helps to break the waste down and makes the soil richer.

Glossary

bristle small, stiff hair that helps a worm to move through the soil

burrow hole than an animal makes in the ground

casting worm's waste

cocoon covering for an egg

segment part of a worm. Most segments of a worm look the same.

soil dirt

Index

Notes for Adults

The *Creepy Creatures* series supports children's growing knowledge and understanding of their world, introducing them to many smaller insects and animals. When used together, the eight books in the series enable comparison of the similarities and differences between these creepy creatures.

These books also help children extend their vocabulary as they hear new words. Since words are used in context in the book, this should enable young children to gradually incorporate them into their own vocabulary. You may like to introduce and explain some new words in this book such as *segments*, *cocoon* and *bristles*.

Additional information
All earthworms are hermaphrodites, which means they have male and female reproductive organs. However, they still need to mate with another earthworm to exchange sperm to fertilize their eggs. The belt-like band on an earthworm's body is called the clitellum. After mating, the clitellum produces a ring of mucus that is used to encase the eggs and sperm. This mucus is used to form a cocoon to protect the developing eggs. There is no larval stage, so the young emerge from the cocoon as tiny adults. Charles Darwin first documented the important role that earthworms play in aerating, mixing, and enriching the soil.

Follow-up activities
• Take children to a nearby park where they can make their own observations about earthworms.
• Talk about what children find interesting about earthworms.
• Encourage children to record their ideas and observations in drawings, paintings, or writing.